W9-BSS-416

A
Treasury
of *Christian*
Prayer

Compiled by Olwen Turchetta
This edition copyright © 2006 Lion Hudson
The compiler asserts the moral right
to be identified as the compiler of this work

All rights reserved. No part of this book may be reproduced or transmitted in any form, or by any means, electronic or mechanical, including photocopying and recording, or by any information storage and retrieval system, without permission in writing from the publisher.

This 2007 edition is published by Testament Books, an imprint of Random House Value Publishing, a division of Random House, Inc., New York, by arrangement with Lion Hudson.

Testament is a registered trademark and the colophon is a trademark of Random House, Inc.

Random House

New York • Toronto • London • Sydney • Auckland

www.valuebooks.com

Typeset in 12/13 Venetian301 BT
Printed and bound in Singapore

A catalog record for this title is available from the Library of Congress.

ISBN: 978-0-517-23049-7

0 9 8 7 6 5 4 3 2 1

Acknowledgments

pp. 9, 13, 30, 46, 50, 72, 86, 91, 95: Extracts from The Book of Common Prayer, the rights in which are vested in the Crown, are reproduced by permission of the Crown's Patentee, Cambridge University Press.

pp 21, 38: from The Prayers and Meditations of Saint Anselm, trans. Benedicta Ward (Penguin Classics 1973). Copyright © Benedicta Ward, 1973.

p. 26: from Early Christian Prayers, edited by A. Hamman, translated by Walter Mitchell, Longman Group.

pp. 32–33 (Lauchlan MacLean Watt), 47 (John Baillie), 94 (Pope John Paul II): from The SPCK Book Of Christian Prayer. Reproduced by permission of Macmillan Ltd.

pp. 33–35, 36–37: from Early Christian Prayers, edited by A. Hamman, translated by Walter Mitchell, Longman Group.

p. 35: from More Everyday Prayers, published by the National Christian Education Council

p. 37: from Family Book of Prayer, Tony Castle, McCrimmons.

pp. 37, 39: The United Society for the Propagation of the Gospel.

p. 38: from Daily Prayer and Praise, by George Appleton, Lutterworth Press. Reproduced by permission of The Lutterworth Press.

p. 52: The Alternative Service Book, 1980, is copyright © The Archbishops' Council. Extract reproduced by permission.

pp. 58, 90: from The Oxford Book of Prayer, edited by George Appleton, 1985, OUP. Reproduced by permission of Oxford University Press.

p. 76: from Praying with St Teresa, SPCK.

pp. 79, 81: from St Francis at Prayer, ed. Wolfgang Bader, Darton, Longman and Todd.

p. 82: from The Glory of Light, by David Adam (2003). Reproduced by permission of SPCK.

p. 89: from The Prayer Manual, edited by F.B. McNutt, 1951, Mowbray. Reproduced by permission of Macmillan Ltd.

A
Treasury
of *Christian*
Prayer

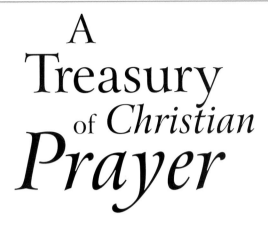

More than 150 Prayers,
Hymns, and Poems

Selected by
Olwen Turchetta

TESTAMENT BOOKS
NEW YORK

To my parents

Contents

Introduction

Having worked as an editor on many prayer books, and experienced the prayer traditions of different denominations during my life, it was a delight to have the opportunity to compile *A Treasury of Christian Prayer*.

As I chose the prayers, I was struck by how many of the same concerns and causes of joy that we have today are found in prayers from centuries ago. While some of the language is more formal, the sentiment is the same. I also find that eloquent language, such as that found in the *Book of Common Prayer*, can add to the beauty of a prayer.

I have chosen prayers from a variety of sources: by well-known saints; from the Celtic tradition; from the liturgy; by Catholic and Protestant writers; by men and women. The common link was that as I read these prayers I felt I could identify with what they were saying. I hope that, whatever tradition you come from, you will find something here that speaks to you.

Olwen Turchetta

Morning
and Night

Morning

Come into my soul, Lord,
as the dawn breaks into the sky;
let your sun rise in my heart
at the coming of the day.

Traditional

O you most holy and ever-loving God, we thank you once more for the quiet rest of the night that has gone by, for the new promise that has come with this fresh morning, and for the hope of this day. While we have slept, the world in which we live has swept on, and we have rested under the shadow of your love. May we trust you this day for all the needs of the body, the soul, and the spirit. Give us this day our daily bread. Amen.

Robert Collyer (19th century)

You wake us to delight in your praises; for you made us for yourself, and our heart is restless until it reposes in you.

St Augustine (354–450)

O Lord, our heavenly Father, Almighty and everlasting God, who hast safely brought us to the beginning of this day; defend us in the same with thy mighty power; and grant that this day we fall into no sin, neither run into any kind of danger; but that all our doings may be ordered by thy governance, to do always that is righteous in thy sight; through Jesus Christ our Lord. Amen

Book of Common Prayer

Lord, thou knowest how busy I must be this day. If I forget thee, do not thou forget me.

Jacob Astley (1579–1652)

Dear God,
In the rush of the morning before a busy day, help us
to remember that whatever we do and wherever we go,
you are always there with us. And when we finally
have time to rest at night, help us to do so, secure in
the knowledge that you will always watch over us
with love.

May the Lord support us all the day long, till the shades lengthen, and the evening comes, and the busy world is hushed, and the fever of life is over, and our work is done! Then in his mercy may he give us safe lodging, a holy rest, and peace at the last.

Attributed to John Henry Newman (1801–90)

O Lord, cause me to hear thy lovingkindness in the morning; for in thee do I trust: cause me to know the way wherein I should walk; for I lift up my soul unto thee.

Psalm 143:8

Lord, may I be wakeful at sunrise to begin a new day for you, cheerful at sunset for having done my work for you; thankful at moonrise and under starshine for the beauty of the universe; and may I add what little may be in me to your great world.

The Abbot of Greve

O make your way plain before my face. Support me this day under all the difficulties I shall meet with. I offer myself to you, O God, this day, to do in me, and with me, as to you seems most meet.

Thomas Wilson (1663–1755)

Dear Lord Jesus, we shall have this day only once; before it is gone, help us to do all the good we can, so that today is not a wasted day.

Stephen Grellet (1773–1855)

O God, who brought me from the rest of last night
To the joyous light of this day,
Bring me from the new light of this day
To the guiding light of eternity.

Carmina Gadelica

Night

We pray thee, O Creator of everything, at this hour preceding night, that thou be clement and watch over us. Let dreams and phantoms of the night be scattered. Keep us safe from our enemy and make us pure!

Attributed to St Ambrose of Milan (340–97)

Preserve us, O Lord, while waking
and guard us while sleeping;
that awake we may watch with Christ,
and asleep we may rest in peace.

A Compline prayer

I am weary, weak and cold,
I am weary of travelling land and sea,
I am weary of travelling moorland and billow,
Grant me peace in the nearness of thy repose this
    night.

Celtic prayer

Lighten our darkness, we beseech thee, O Lord;
and by thy great mercy defend us from all perils and
dangers of this night; for the love of thy only Son,
our Saviour, Jesus Christ. Amen.

Book of Common Prayer

We thank thee, our heavenly Father, through Jesus Christ, thy dear Son, that thou hast graciously kept us this day; and we pray thee that thou wouldst forgive us all our sins where we have done wrong, and graciously keep us this night. For into thy hands we commend ourselves, our bodies and souls, and all things. Let thy holy angel be with us, that the wicked foe may have no power over us.

Martin Luther (1483–1546)

O God,
May there be nothing in this day's
work of which we shall be ashamed
when the sun has set, nor in the
eventide of our life when our task is
done and we go to our long home to
meet you face to face. Amen.

Walter Rauschenbusch (1861–1918)

O eternal God and ruler of all
creation, you have allowed me to reach
this hour. Forgive the sins I have
committed this day by word, deed or
thought. Purify me, O Lord, from
every spiritual and physical stain.
Grant that I may rise from this sleep
to glorify you by my deeds throughout
my entire lifetime, and that I be
victorious over every spiritual and
physical enemy. Deliver me, O Lord,
from all vain thoughts and from evil
desires, for yours is the kingdom, the
power, and the glory, Father, Son and
Holy Spirit, now and for ever. Amen.

St Macarius of Egypt (c. 300–c. 90)

The Lord almighty grant us a quiet
night and a perfect end.

A Compline prayer

I lie down this night with God,
And God will lie down with me;
I lie down this night with Christ,
And Christ will lie down with me;
I lie down this night with the Spirit,
And the Spirit will lie down with me;
God and Christ and the Spirit
Be lying down with me.

Carmina Gadelica

Joy and
Praise

O come, let us sing unto the Lord:
let us make a joyful noise to the rock of our salvation.
Let us come before his presence with thanksgiving,
and make a joyful noise unto him with psalms.
For the Lord is a great God,
and a great King above all gods.
In his hand are the deep places of the earth:
the strength of the hills is his also.
The sea is his, and he made it:
and his hands formed the dry land.
O come, let us worship and bow down:
let us kneel before the Lord our maker.

Psalm 95:1–6

O most high, almighty, good Lord, God:
to you belong praise, glory, honour and all blessing.
Praised be my Lord by all his creatures,
and chiefly by our brother the sun,
who brings us the day and the light.
Fair is he, and shines with a very great splendour:
O Lord, he points us to you.
Praised be my Lord by our sister the moon,
and by the stars which you have set clear and lovely
    in heaven.
Praised be my Lord by our brother the wind,
and by air and cloud, calms and all weather,
by which you uphold life in all creatures.

Praised be my Lord by our sister water,
who is very useful to us and humble and precious
    and clean.
Praised be my Lord by our brother fire,
through whom you give light in the darkness;
and he is bright and pleasant and very mighty and
    strong.
Praised be my Lord by our mother the earth,
who sustains us and keeps us,
and brings forth fruits of different kinds, flowers
    of many colours and grass.

St Francis of Assisi (1181–1226)

Lord, you are to be blessed and praised;
all good things come from you:
you are in our words and in our thoughts,
and in all that we do.
Amen.

St Teresa of Avila (1515–82)

Grant to us, O Lord, the royalty of inward happiness,
and the serenity which comes from living close to thee.
Daily renew in us the sense of joy, and let the eternal
Spirit of the Father dwell in our souls and bodies,
filling every corner of our hearts with light and grace;
so that, bearing about with us the infection of good
courage, we may be diffusers of life, and may meet all
ills and cross accidents with gallant and high-hearted
happiness, giving thee thanks always for all things.

Robert Louis Stevenson (1850–94)

My God,
I pray that I may so know you and love you
    that I may rejoice in you.
And if I may not do so fully in this life,
    let me go steadily on
    to the day when I come to that fullness…
    let me receive
That which you promised through your truth,
    that my joy may be full.

St Anselm (1033–1109)

May none of God's wonderful works keep silence,
night or morning.
Bright stars, high mountains, the depths of the seas,
sources of rushing rivers:
may all these break into song as we sing
to Father, Son and Holy Spirit.
May all the angels in the heavens reply:
Amen! Amen! Amen!
Power, praise, honour, eternal glory to God,
the only Giver of grace.
Amen! Amen! Amen!

Third-century hymn

I will greatly rejoice in the Lord, my soul shall be
joyful in my God; for he hath clothed me with the
garments of salvation, he hath covered me with the
robe of righteousness.

Isaiah 61:10

My soul doth magnify the Lord,
and my spirit hath rejoiced in God my Saviour.
For he hath regarded
the lowliness of his handmaiden.
For behold, from henceforth,
all generations shall call me blessed.
For he that is mighty hath magnified me,
and holy is his name.
And his mercy is on them that fear him
throughout all generations.
He hath shewed strength with his arm:
he hath scattered the proud in the imagination of
  their hearts.
He hath put down the mighty from their seat,
and hath exalted the humble and meek.
He hath filled the hungry with good things,
and the rich he hath sent empty away.
He, remembering his mercy, hath holpen his servant
  Israel,
as he promised to our forefathers, Abraham, and his
  seed, for ever.

The Magnificat (Luke 1:46–55)

Let our mouths be filled with thy praise, O Lord,
that we may sing of thy glory, because thou hast
counted us worthy to partake of thy holy, divine,
immortal and life-giving mysteries: preserve us in thy
holiness, that we may learn of thy righteousness all
the day long. Alleluia, alleluia, alleluia.

Liturgy of St John Chrysostom and St Basil the Great

Blessings and honour and thanksgiving and praise,
more than we can utter, more than we can conceive,
be unto thee, O holy and glorious Trinity, Father,
Son, and Holy Ghost, by all angels, by all men, all
creatures, for ever and ever.

Thomas Ken (1637–1711)

You are holy, Lord, the only God,
  and your deeds are wonderful.
You are strong.
  You are great.
  You are Most High,
  You are almighty.
  You, holy Father, are
  King of heaven and earth.
You are Three and One,
  Lord God, all good.
  You are Good, all Good, supreme
  Good,
  Lord God, living and true.
You are love,
  You are wisdom.
  You are humility,
  You are endurance.
  You are rest,
  You are peace.
  You are joy and gladness.
  You are justice and moderation.
  You are all our riches,
  And you suffice for us.
You are beauty.

You are gentleness.
You are our protector,
You are our guardian and defender.
You are courage.
You are our haven and our hope.
You are our faith,
   Our great consolation.
   You are our eternal life,
   Great and wonderful Lord,
   God almighty,
   Merciful Saviour.

St Francis of Assisi (1181–1226)

O God, our true life, to know you is life, to serve you is freedom, to enjoy you is a kingdom, to praise you is the joy and happiness of the soul. I praise and bless and adore you, I worship you, I glorify you. I give thanks to you for your great glory. I humbly beg you to live with me, to reign in me, to make this heart of mine a holy temple, a fit habitation for your divine majesty.

St Augustine (354–430)

Glory to God for all things!

St John Chrysostom (c. 347–407)

Thou art never weary, O Lord, of doing us good. Let us never be weary of doing thee service. But, as thou hast pleasure in the prosperity of thy servants, so let us take pleasure in the service of our Lord, and abound in thy work, and in thy love and praise evermore. O fill up all that is wanting, reform whatever is amiss in us, perfect the thing that concerneth us. Let the witness of thy pardoning love ever abide in all our hearts.

John Wesley (1703–91)

Praise ye the Lord. Praise God in his sanctuary: praise him in the firmament of his power.
Praise him for his mighty acts: praise him according to his excellent greatness.
Praise him with the sound of the trumpet: praise him with the psaltery and harp.

Praise him with the timbrel and dance: praise him
   with stringed instruments and organs.
Praise him upon the loud cymbals: praise him upon
   the high sounding cymbals.
Let every thing that hath breath praise the Lord.
Praise ye the Lord.

Psalm 150

We praise thee, O God: we acknowledge thee to be
the Lord.
All the earth doth worship thee, the Father everlasting.
To thee all Angels cry aloud: the Heavens, and all the
powers therein.
To thee Cherubim and Seraphim continually do cry,
Holy, Holy, Holy, Lord God of Sabaoth;
Heaven and earth are full of thy Majesty, of thy
Glory.
The glorious company of the Apostles praise thee.
The goodly fellowship of the Prophets praise thee.
The noble army of Martyrs praise thee.
The holy Church throughout all the world doth
acknowledge thee;
The Father of an infinite Majesty;
Thine honourable, true and only Son;
Also the Holy Ghost: the Comforter.

Te deum laudamus, Book of Common Prayer

Sing, O heavens; and be joyful, O earth; and break
forth into singing, O mountains: for the Lord hath
comforted his people, and will have mercy upon his
afflicted.

Isaiah 49:13

Dear God,
Grant us the perfect joy that comes from praising
you with a true heart.

God, I give you the praise for days well spent. But I am yet unsatisfied, because I do not enjoy enough of you. I apprehend myself at too great a distance from you. I would have my soul more closely united to you by faith and love.

You know, Lord, that I would love you above all things. You made me; you know my desires, my expectations. My joys all centre in you and it is you that I desire. It is your favour, your acceptance, the communications of your grace that I earnestly wish for more than anything in the world.

I rejoice in your essential glory and blessedness. I rejoice in my relation to you, that you are my Father, my Lord and my God. I thank you that you have brought me so far. I will beware of despairing of your mercy for the time which is yet to come, and will give you the glory of your free grace.

Susanna Wesley (1669–1742)

Glorious Lord, I give you greeting!
Let the church and the chancel praise you,
Let the plain and the hillside praise you,
Let the dark and daylight praise you,
Let the birds and the honeybees praise you,
Let the male and the female praise you,
And I shall praise you, Lord of glory:
Glorious Lord, I give you greeting!

Welsh prayer

May the Lord be blessed for ever for the great
  gifts
that he has continually heaped upon me,
and may all that he has created praise him. Amen.

St Teresa of Avila (1515–82)

Glory be to the Father and to the Son and to
the Holy Ghost. As it was in the beginning, is
now, and ever shall be, world without end. Amen.

Book of Common Prayer

Intercession

Grant us grace, Almighty Father, so to pray as to deserve to be heard.

Jane Austen (1775–1827)

Almighty God, who hast given us grace at this time with one accord to make our common supplications unto thee; and dost promise that when two or three are gathered together in thy name thou wilt grant their requests: fulfil now, O Lord, the desires and petitions of thy servants, as may be most expedient for them; granting us in this world knowledge of thy truth, and in the world to come life everlasting.

St John Chrysostom (c. 347–407)

O Lord, we pray for the universal church, for all sections of your church throughout the world, for their truth, unity and stability, that love may abound and truth flourish in them all.

We pray for our own church, that what is lacking in it may be supplied and what is unsound corrected; and unto all men everywhere give your grace and your blessing; for the sake of Jesus Christ, our only Lord and Saviour.

Lancelot Andrewes (1555–1626)

Hasten thou, O Christ, that day when every heart shall know and love thee, the Lord. Bless thy holy Church throughout the earth. Free her from narrowness, bigotry, and pride of self. Throw her doors wide to the wall, deepen her thought, broaden her sympathies, till she shall be as thou art, shelter and home, and shield and dwelling-place, of all the weary and the wandering that are seeking rest.

Lauchlan MacLean Watt (1867–1957)

Dear God, we pray for the church and for the world. Help the different branches of the church to look for the things that unite, not those that divide, and to bear witness to your love in the world.

We pray for our country and all the countries of the world. May all rulers and leaders govern according to your laws of justice and peace.

We pray for all those known and unknown to us who are suffering or in need. Be close to them, O Lord, and guide them through this time.

We pray for all those who have died. Eternal rest grant unto them, O Lord. Let perpetual light shine upon them; may they rest in peace.

We ask this and all our prayers through Christ, our Lord. Amen.

To those who rule and lead us on the earth, you, sovereign Master, have given their authority and kingship – so marvellous that power of yours words fail to express – that seeing the glory and honour, You have have provided for them, we should be subject to their rule, not resisting your will. Grant

them, Lord, the health, peace, concord and stability
to use aright the sovereignty you have bestowed on
them. For you, King of heaven, you it is that give
mortal men glory, honour and power over what is
on earth. Lord, make their counsels conform to

what is good and pleasing to you, that using with
reverence, peacefully, gently, the power you have
given them, they may find favour with you.

St Clement of Rome (first century)

Father, from whom every family receives its true name,
I pray for all the members of my family:
for those who are growing up,
that they may increase in wisdom and love;
for those facing changes,
that they may meet them with hope;
for those who are weak,
that they may find strength;
for those with heavy burdens,
that they may carry them lightly;
for those who are old and frail,
that they may grow in faith.

From *More Everyday Prayers*

Comfort, O merciful Father, by thy Word and Holy
Spirit, all who are afflicted or distressed, and so turn
their hearts unto thee, that they may serve thee in
truth and bring forth fruit to thy glory. Be thou, O
Lord, their succour and defence, through Jesus Christ
our Lord.

Philip Melanchthon (1497–1560)

We beg you, Lord, to help and defend us. Deliver the oppressed, pity the insignificant, raise the fallen, show yourself to the needy, heal the sick, bring back those of your people who have gone astray, feed the hungry, lift up the weak, take off the prisoners' chains.

May every nation come to know that you alone are God, that Jesus Christ is your child, that we are your people, the sheep that you pasture.

St Clement of Rome (first century)

O living bread, that came down from heaven to give life to the world! O loving shepherd of our souls… we commend to you particularly the sick, the unhappy, the poor and all who beg for food and employment, imploring for all and every one the assistance of your providence; we commend to you the families, so that they may be fruitful centres of Christian life. May the abundance of your grace be poured out over all.

Pope John XXIII (1881–1963)

O Christ, bless and uphold all who are in pain or sickness this day.

United Society for the Propagation of the Gospel

God of love, whose compassion never fails; we bring before thee the troubles and perils of people and nations, the sighing of prisoners and captives, the sorrows of the bereaved, the necessities of strangers, the helplessness of the weak, the despondency of the weary, the failing powers of the aged. O Lord, draw near to each; for the sake of Jesus Christ our Lord.

St Anselm (1033–1109)

O merciful and loving Father of all, look down we pray thee on the many millions who are hungry in the world today and at the mercy of disease. Grant that we who have lived so comfortably and gently all our lives may have true sympathy with them and do all in our power, as individuals and as a nation, to help them to that abundant life which is thy will for them; through Jesus Christ our Lord.

George Appleton

O God, we pray for those who do not know you, or who do not believe in you. Help us to show you to them through the lives that we lead, so that we may help them to discover the joy of knowing you.

The things, good Lord, that we pray for, give us grace to work for; through Jesus Christ our Lord.

Thomas More (1478–1535)

O blessed Lord, who has commanded us to love one another, grant us grace that having received your undeserved bounty, we may love everyone in you and for you. We implore your clemency for all; but especially for the friends whom your love has given to us. Love them, O fountain of love, and make them love you with all their heart, that they may will and speak and do those things only which are pleasing to you.

St Anselm (1033–1109)

Lord, thou knowest what I want,
if it be thy will that I have it,
and if it be not thy will,
good Lord, do not be displeased,
for I want nothing which you do not want.

Julian of Norwich (1342–c. 1416)

O God, who art present to thy people in every place, mercifully hear our prayers for those we love who are now parted from us: watch over them, we beseech thee, and protect them from anxiety, danger and temptation; and assure both them and us that thou art always near, and that we are one in thee for ever; through Jesus Christ our Lord.

Brooke Foss Westcott (1825–1901)

Heavenly Father, we beseech thee to look in thy mercy upon this household. Grant that every member of it may be taught and guided by thee. Bless the relations and friends of each of us: thou knowest their several necessities; and prosper our efforts to advance thy kingdom at home and abroad; for our Lord Jesus Christ's sake.

Archibald Campbell Tait (1811–82)

O Christ, be with all who are facing death today in fear or loneliness.

United Society for the Propagation of the Gospel

Remember, O Lord, we beseech thee, the souls of
them that have kept the faith, both those whom we
remember and those whom we remember not; and
grant them rest in the land of the living, in the joy
of Paradise, whence all pain and grief have fled away;
where the light of thy countenance shineth for ever;

and guide in peace the end of our lives, O Lord,
when thou wilt and as thou wilt, only without shame
and sin; through thine only-begotten Son, our Lord
and Saviour, Jesus Christ.

Liturgy of St John Chrysostom and St Basil the Great

Be gracious to all that are near and dear to me and keep us all in thy fear and love. Guide us, good Lord, and govern us by the same Spirit, that we may be so united to thee here as not to be divided when you are pleased to call us hence, but may together enter into thy glory, through Jesus Christ, our blessed Lord and Saviour.

John Wesley (1703–91)

Look upon us, O Lord,
and let all the darkness of our souls vanish
before the beams of thy brightness.
Fill us with holy love,
and open to us the treasures of thy wisdom.
All our desire is known unto thee,
therefore perfect what thou hast begun,
and what thy Spirit has awakened us to ask in prayer.
We seek thy face,
turn thy face unto us and show us thy glory.
Then shall our longing be satisfied,
and our peace shall be perfect.

St Augustine (354–430)

Confession

Almighty and merciful God, the fountain of all
goodness, who knowest the thoughts of our hearts,
we confess unto thee that we have sinned against
thee, and done evil in thy sight. Wash us, we beseech
thee, from the stains of our past sins, and give us
grace and power to put away all hurtful things; so
that, being delivered from the bondage of sin, we
may bring forth worthy fruits of repentance, through
Jesus Christ, our Lord.

Alcuin (735–804)

O God, our Judge and Saviour, set before us the vision of your purity and let us see our sins in the light of your holiness. Pierce our self-contentment with the shafts of your burning love and let love consume in us all that hinders us from perfect service of your cause; for your holiness is our judgement, so are your wounds our salvation.

William Temple (1881–1944)

Save me, Lord, King of eternal glory, you who have the power to save us all. Grant that I may long for, do and perfect those things which are pleasing to you and profitable for me. Lord, give me counsel in my anxiety, help in time of trial, solace when persecuted and strength against every temptation. Grant me pardon, Lord, for my past wrongdoings and afflictions, correction of my present ones and deign also to protect me against those in the future.

Latin prayer (11th century)

Create in me a clean heart, O God;
and renew a right spirit within me.
Cast me not away from thy presence;
and take not thy holy spirit from me.

Psalm 51:10, 11

I have gone astray like a lost sheep; seek thy servant; for I do not forget thy commandments.

Psalm 119:176

Almighty and most merciful Father; we have erred, and strayed from thy ways like lost sheep. We have followed too much the devices and desires of our own hearts. We have offended against thy holy laws. We have left undone those things which we ought to have done; and we have done those things which we ought not to have done; and there is no health in us. But thou, O Lord, have mercy upon us, miserable offenders. Spare thou them, O God, which confess their faults. Restore thou them that are penitent; according to thy promises declared unto mankind in Christ Jesu our Lord. And grant, O most merciful Father, for his sake; that we may hereafter live a godly, righteous, and sober life, to the glory of thy holy Name. Amen.

Book of Common Prayer

O Lord, who hast mercy upon all, take away from me my sins, and mercifully kindle in me the fire of thy Holy Spirit. Take away from me the heart of stone, and give me a heart of flesh, a heart to love and adore thee, a heart to delight in thee, to follow and to enjoy thee, for Christ's sake.

St Ambrose of Milan (c. 339–97)

Be not wroth very sore, O Lord, neither remember iniquity for ever: behold, see, we beseech thee, we are all thy people.

Isaiah 64:9

O most merciful Father, who dost put away the sins of those who truly repent, we come before thy throne in the name of Jesus Christ, that for his sake alone thou wilt have compassion upon us, and let not our sins be a cloud between thee and us.

John Colet (1467–1519)

For my deceitful heart and crooked thoughts:
For barbed words spoken deliberately:
For thoughtless words spoken hastily:
For envious and prying eyes:
For ears that rejoice in iniquity and rejoice not in
   the truth:
For greedy hands:
For wandering and loitering feet:
For haughty looks:
Have mercy upon me, O God.

John Baillie (1886–1960)

O Lord,
Forgive us if any hours have been wasted on profitless things that have brought us no satisfaction, or if we have dragged our dusty cares into your sacred day and made the holy common.

Walter Rauschenbusch (1816–1918)

Forgive me, Lord, my sins – the sins of my youth, the sins of the present; the sins I laid upon myself in an ill pleasure, the sins I cast upon others in an ill example; the sins which are manifest to all the world, the sins which I have laboured to hide from mine acquaintance, from mine own conscience, and even from my memory; my crying sins and my whispering sins, my ignorant sins and my wilful; sins against my superiors, equals, servants, against my lovers and benefactors, sins against myself, mine own body, mine own soul, sins against thee, O almighty Father, O merciful Son, O blessed Spirit of God.

Forgive me, O Lord, through the merits of thine anointed, my Saviour, Jesus Christ.

John Donne (1573–1631)

Dear God,
I think of all the opportunities I missed today: the chance to offer support to someone in need; to think of others before myself; to do good rather than looking the other way. Please help me to see the opportunities tomorrow.

I am heartily sorry, and beg pardon for my sins, especially for my little respect, and for wandering in my thoughts when in your presence, and for my continual infidelitys to your graces; for all which I beg pardon, by the merits of the Blood you shed for them.

Lady Lucy Herbert (1669–1744)

O Lord our God, grant us grace to desire you with our whole heart, that so desiring you we may seek you and find you; and so finding you, we may love you; and loving you we may hate those sins from which you have redeemed us; for the sake of Jesus Christ.

St Anselm (1033–1109)

All that we ought to have thought and have not
  thought,
All that we ought to have said and have not said,
All that we ought to have done and have not done,
All that we ought not to have spoken and yet have
  spoken,
All that we ought not to have done and yet have
  done,
For these words and works, pray we, O God, for
forgiveness.

> Traditional

O Lord, I beseech thee to pardon those sins which
I have committed during this day. Not only those
unkind or selfish acts that I have done, or cruel
words that I have said, but also the many thoughts
that are contrary to what is right and good. In thy
mercy, forgive me my hypocrisy, my jealousy and my
carelessness. Help me not only to turn away from
that which is wrong, but to see all the things I could
do for the good of others every day of my life.

Remember not, Lord, our offences, nor the offences
of our forefathers; neither take thou vengeance of our
sins: spare us, good Lord, spare thy people, whom
thou hast redeemed with thy most precious blood,
and be not angry with us for ever.

> From the Litany, Book of Common Prayer

O thou great Chief, light a candle in my heart, that I may see what is therein, and sweep the rubbish from thy dwelling place.

An African schoolgirl's prayer

Lord Jesus Christ, Son of God, have mercy on me, a sinner.

Eastern Orthodox

Almighty and everlasting God,
you hate nothing that you have made
and forgive the sins of all those who are penitent.
Create and make in us new and contrite hearts,
that, lamenting our sins
and acknowledging our wretchedness,
we may receive from you, the God of all mercy,
perfect forgiveness and peace;
through Jesus Christ our Lord.

The Alternative Service Book, 1980

Thankfulness

Dear God,
Thank you for all the ways we see you in the world:
  through the beauty of your creation,
  through music and art,
  through the love of friends and family.
But thank you above all for your Son, and the love
  you showed us through him.

Give thanks to the Lord, for he is good;
his love endures for ever.

Psalm 118:1

We worship you, O Lord God, and give thanks to
you for your great glory and power, which you show
to your servants in your wonderful world. All the
things which we enjoy are from your mighty hand,
and you alone are to be praised for all the blessings
of the life that now is. Make us thankful to you for
all your mercies and more ready to serve you with all
our heart; for the sake of Jesus Christ. Amen.

From *The Narrow Way* (1869)

We adore you, Lord Jesus Christ,
in all the churches of the whole world
and we bless you, for by means of your holy cross
you have redeemed the world.

St Francis of Assisi (1182–1226)

O you who are the God of all the generations of
men, we thank you for all who have walked humbly
with you and especially those near to us and dear, in
whose lives we have seen the vision of your beauty.
May we know that in the body or out of the body
they are with you. Unite us still, God of our souls, in
one household of faith and love, one family in heaven
and on earth; through Jesus Christ our Lord.

John Hunter (1849–1917)

I thank thee, O Lord, my Lord,
   for my being,
      my life,
      my gift of reason;
   for my nurture,
      my preservation,
      my guidance;
   for my education,
      my civil rights,
      my religious privileges;
   for thy gifts of grace,
      of nature,
      of this world;
   for my redemption,
      my regeneration,
      my instruction in the Christian faith;
   for my calling,
      my recalling,
      my manifold renewed recalling;
   for thy forbearance and long-suffering,
      thy prolonged forbearance, many a time,
      and many a year;
   for all the benefits I have received,
      and all the undertakings wherein I have prospered;
   for any good I may have done;
   for the use of the blessings of this life;
   for thy promise,
      and my hope of the enjoyment of good things to
      come;
   ... for all these and also for all other mercies,
known and unknown,
open and secret,

remembered by me, or now forgotten,
kindnesses received by me willingly, or
even against my will,
I praise thee, I bless thee, I thank thee,
all the days of my life.

Lancelot Andrewes (1555–1626)

For all the rich autumnal glories spread –
the flaming pageant of the ripening woods,
the fiery gorse, the heather-purpled hills;
the rustling leaves that fly before the wind
and lie below the hedgerows whispering;
for meadows silver-white with hoary dew;
the first crisp breath of wonder in the air,
we thank you, Lord.

Anonymous

O God our Father, we would thank thee for all the
bright things of life. Help us to see them, and to
count them, and to remember them, that our lives
may flow in ceaseless praise; for the sake of Jesus
Christ our Lord.

J. H. Jowett (1846–1923)

O God, I thank thee
for all the creatures thou hast made,
so perfect in their kind –
great animals like the elephant and the rhinoceros,
humorous animals like the camel and the monkey,
friendly ones like the dog and the cat,
working ones like the horse and the ox,
timid ones like the squirrel and the rabbit,
majestic ones like the lion and the tiger,
for birds with their songs.
O Lord, give us such love for thy creation,
that love may cast out fear,
and all thy creatures see in man
their priest and friend,
through Jesus Christ our Lord.

George Appleton

O God, we thank you for this earth, our home; for the wide sky and the blessed sun, for the salt sea and the running water, for the everlasting hills and the never-resting winds, for trees and the common grass underfoot.

We thank you for our senses by which we hear the songs of birds, and see the splendour of the summer fields, and taste of the autumn fruits, and rejoice in the feel of the snow, and smell the breath of the spring.

Grant us a heart wide open to all this beauty; and save our souls from being so blind that we pass unseeing when even the common thornbush is aflame with your glory, O God our creator, who lives and reigns for ever and ever.

Walter Rauschenbusch (1861–1918)

Almighty God, we offer unto you most high praise and hearty thanks for the wonderful graces and virtues which you have manifested in all your saints and in all other holy persons upon earth, who by their lives and labours have shined forth as lights in the world, whom we remember with honour and commemorate with joy. For these and for all your other servants who have departed this life with the seal of faith, we praise and magnify your holy name; through Jesus Christ our Lord.

From the Scottish Liturgy (1560)

O Lord, that lends me life,
Lend me a heart replete with thankfulness.

William Shakespeare (1564–1616)

Thou hast given so much to me,
Give one thing more – a grateful heart;
Not thankful when it pleases me,
As if thy blessings had spare days;
But such a heart whose very pulse may be
Thy praise.

George Herbert (1593–1633)

We thank thee, Lord, for the glory of the late days
and the excellent face of thy sun. We thank thee for
good news received. We thank thee for the pleasures
we have enjoyed and for those we have been able to
confer. And now, when the clouds gather and rain
impends over the forest and our house, permit us not
to be cast down; let us not lose the savour of past
mercies and past pleasures; but, like the voice of a
bird singing in the rain, let grateful memory survive
in the hour of darkness.

Robert Louis Stevenson (1850–94)

O God,
We give thanks for the goodhearted people who love
us and do good to us and who show their mercy and
kindness by providing us with food and drink, house
and shelter when we are in trouble or in need.

From a 1739 prayer book

We thank thee, O God, for the saints of all ages; for those who in times of darkness kept the lamp of faith burning; for the great souls who saw visions of larger truth and dared to declare it; for the multitude of quiet and gracious souls whose presence has purified and sanctified the world; and for those known and loved by us, who have passed from this earthly fellowship into the fuller light of life with thee.

Anonymous

It is very meet and right, just and for salvation, that
we should at all times and in all places give thanks
unto thee: O Lord, holy Father, almighty everlasting
God: because through the mystery of the incarnate
Word the light of thy glory hath shone anew upon
the eyes of our mind: that while we acknowledge God
made visible, we may be caught up through him to
the love of things invisible. And therefore with angels
and archangels, with thrones and dominations and
with all the host of the heavenly army we sing the
hymn of thy glory, evermore saying: Holy, Holy, Holy
Lord God of Hosts, Heaven and earth are full of thy
glory. Hosanna in the highest. Blessed is he who
cometh in the name of the Lord. Hosanna in the
highest.

Preface of the Nativity, Roman Rite

Lord God, thank you for loving us
even when we turn away from you.
We are grateful for your constant care and concern.
Though we feel unworthy of your great love,
we thank you that through our weaknesses you give
    us strength;
and in our wanderings you show us the way.

Author unknown

Dear God, thank you that, whatever we have done
and however far from you we have strayed, it is never
too late to turn back to you. Your love is so great
that you will always welcome those who come to you.

Thank you, Lord Jesus, that you will be our hiding place whatever happens.

Corrie ten Boom (1892–1983)

Thanks be to thee, O Lord Jesus Christ,
for all the benefits which thou hast won for us,
for all the pains and insults which thou hast borne
   for us.
O most merciful redeemer,
friend and brother,
may we know thee more clearly, love thee more dearly,
and follow thee more nearly, day by day.

Richard of Chichester (1197–1253)

Guidance

God be in my head, and in my understanding,
God be in mine eyes, and in my looking,
God be in my mouth, and in my speaking,
God be in my heart, and in my thinking,
God be at my end, and at my departing.

Sarum Primer (1527)

My dearest Lord,
be thou a bright flame before me,
be thou a guiding star above me,
be thou a smooth path beneath me,
be thou a kindly shepherd behind me,
today and for evermore.

St Columba (521–97)

Grant, O God, your protection; and in your
protection, strength; and in strength, understanding;
and in understanding, knowledge; and in knowledge,
the knowledge of justice; and in the knowledge of
justice, the love of it; and in that love, the love of
existence; and in the love of existence, the love of
God and of all goodness.

Source unknown (early Welsh)

Christ with me sleeping,
Christ with me waking,
Christ with me watching,
Each day and night.
God with me protecting,
The Lord with me directing,
The Spirit with me strengthening,
For ever and for evermore.

Carmina Gadelica

God, I want thy guidance and direction in all I do.
Let thy wisdom counsel me, thy hand lead me, and
thine arm support me. I put myself into thy hands.
Breathe into my soul holy and heavenly desires.
Conform me to thine own image. Make me like my
Saviour. Enable me in some measure to live here on
earth as he lived, and to act in all things as he would
have acted.

Ashton Oxenden (1808–92)

May the strength of God pilot us,
May the power of God preserve us,
May the wisdom of God instruct us,
May the hand of God protect us,
May the way of God direct us,
May the shield of God defend us,
May the host of God guard us against the snares
   of evil
and the temptations of the world.

St Patrick (c. 389–c. 461)

O Lord, put no trust in me, for I shall surely fall
if you uphold me not.

St Philip Neri (1515–95)

O God, grant us the serenity
to accept what cannot be changed,
the courage to change what can be changed
and the wisdom to know the difference.

Reinbold Niebuhr (1892–1971)

God guide me with your wisdom,
God chastise me with your justice,
God help me with your mercy,
God protect me with your strength.
God fill me with your fullness,
God shield me with your shade,
God fill me with your grace,
For the sake of your anointed Son.

Carmina Gadelica

O Lord, whose way is perfect, help us, we pray,
always to trust in your goodness, that walking with
you and following you in all simplicity, we may
possess quiet and contented minds and may cast all
our care on you, who cares for us. Grant this, O
Lord, for your dear Son's sake, Jesus Christ.

Christina Rossetti (1830–94)

Dear God,
Lead us in your ways during our life on earth. Then,
when our time has come, lead us home to your glory.

Father,
I am seeking:
I am hesitant and uncertain,
but will you, O God,
watch over each step of mine
and guide me.

St Augustine (354–430)

Grant to me, O Lord, to know what I ought to know,
to love what I ought to love, to praise what delights
thee most, to value what is precious in thy sight, to
hate what is offensive to thee. Do not suffer me to
judge according to the sight of my eyes, nor to pass
sentence according to the hearing of the ears of
ignorant men; but to discern with true judgement
between things visible and spiritual, and above all
things to enquire what is the good pleasure of thy will.

Thomas à Kempis (1380–1471)

Whoever truly loves you, good Lord,
walks in safety down a royal road, far from the
    dangerous abyss;
and if he so much as stumbles, you, O Lord, stretch
    out your hand.
Not one fall, or many, will cause you to abandon him
    if he loves you
and does not love the things of this world,
because he walks in the vale of humility.

St Teresa of Avila (1515–82)

Be, Lord, within me to strengthen me, without me to preserve, over me to shelter, beneath me to support, before me to direct, behind me to bring back, round about me to fortify.

Lancelot Andrewes (1555–1626)

O God, I will not fear. Thou art with me: I will not be dismayed. Thou art my God and wilt strenghten me and wilt help me. Thou wilt uphold me with the right hand of thy righteousness.

Adapted from Isaiah 41:10

Alone with none but thee, my God,
I journey on my way.
What need I fear, when thou art near
O King of night and day?
More safe am I within thy hand
Than if a host did round me stand.

St Columba (521–97)

Our Father, who art in heaven,
hallowed be thy name;
thy kingdom come;
thy will be done;
on earth as it is in heaven.
Give us this day our daily bread.
And forgive us our trespasses,
as we forgive those who trespass against us.
And lead us not into temptation;
but deliver us from evil.
For thine is the kingdom,
the power and the glory,
for ever and ever.
Amen.

Traditional version, Book of Common Prayer

O God, help me to remember that there is a purpose to everything in life, and to trust in you when things don't happen as I expect. Guide me through the times in my life when I feel there is no direction, and help me to trust that all will turn out for the good even if it is different from what I had planned.

O God, by whom the meek are guided in judgement, and whose light rises up in darkness for the godly; give us, in all our doubts and uncertainties, the grace to ask what thou wouldst have us to do; that the spirit of wisdom may save us from all false choices, and that in thy light we may see light and in thy straight path may not stumble; through Jesus Christ our Lord.

William Bright (1824–1901)

Lead kindly light, amid the encircling gloom,
Lead thou me on;
The night is dark, and I am far from home;
Lead thou me on.
Keep thou my feet; I do not ask to see
The distant scene; one step enough for me.

John Henry Newman (1801–90)

The Lord is my shepherd; I shall not want.
He maketh me to lie down in green pastures: he
leadeth me beside the still waters.
He restoreth my soul: he leadeth me in the paths of
righteousness for his name's sake.
Yea, though I walk through the valley of the shadow
of death, I will fear no evil: for thou art with me; thy
rod and thy staff they comfort me.

Thou preparest a table before me in the presence of mine enemies: thou anointest my head with oil; my cup runneth over.

Surely goodness and mercy shall follow me all the days of my life: and I will dwell in the house of the Lord for ever.

Psalm 23

Let us make our way together, Lord: wherever you go I must go; and through whatever you pass, there too will I pass.

St Teresa of Avila (1515–82)

O heavenly Father, in whom we live and move and have our being, we humbly pray you so to guide and govern us by your Holy Spirit that in all the cares and occupations of our daily life we may never forget you, but remember that we are ever walking in your sight; for your own name's sake.

Ancient collect

Suffering and
Healing

I am here abroad,
I am here in need,
I am here in pain,
I am here in straits,
I am here alone,
O God, aid me.

Carmina Gadelica

O God, from whom to be turned is to fall,
to whom to be turned is to rise,
and in whom to stand is to abide for ever;
grant us in all our duties thy help,
in all our perplexities thy guidance,
in all our dangers thy protection,
and in all our sorrows thy peace;
through Jesus Christ our Lord.

St Augustine (354–430)

Give us patience and steadfastness in adversity,
strengthen our weakness, comfort us in trouble and
distress, help us to fight; grant unto us that in true
obedience and contentation of mind we may give over
our own wills unto thee our Father in all things,
according to the example of thy beloved Son; that in
adversity we grudge not, but offer up ourselves unto
thee without contradiction… Give us a willing and
cheerful mind, that we may gladly suffer and bear all
things for thy sake.

Miles Coverdale (1488–1568)

I thank you, Lord God,
for all my pains;
if it please you, Lord,
increase them a hundredfold.
I shall thankfully accept
whatever sorrow you give, not sparing me;
for in the fulfilment of your will
I find my greatest solace.

St Francis of Assisi (1182–1226)

Almighty and merciful God, who art the strength of
the weak, the refreshment of the weary, the comfort
of the sad, the help of the tempted, the life of the
dying, the God of patience and of all consolation;
thou knowest full well the inner weakness of our
nature, how we tremble and quiver before pain, and
cannot bear the cross without thy divine help and
support. Help me, then, O eternal and pitying God,
help me to possess my soul in patience, to maintain
unshaken hope in thee, to keep that childlike trust
which feels a Father's heart hidden beneath the cross;
so shall I be strengthened with power according to
thy glorious might, in all patience and long-suffering;
I shall be enabled to endure pain and temptation,
and, in the very depth of my suffering, to praise thee
with a joyful heart.

Johann Habermann (1516–90)

Teach us, Lord,
to serve you as you deserve,
to give and not to count the cost,
to fight and not to heed the wounds,
to toil and not to seek for rest,
to labour and not to seek for any reward
save that of knowing that we do your will.

St Ignatius Loyola (1491–1556)

Heal us, Lord, and we shall be healed; save us and
we shall be saved; for it is you we praise. Send relief
and healing for our diseases, our sufferings and our
wounds; for you are a merciful and faithful healer.
Blessed are you, Lord, who heals the sick.

A Jewish prayer

Lord, look down on me in my infirmities
and help me to bear them patiently.

St Francis of Assisi (1182–1226)

Watch, dear Lord, with those who wake, or watch,
   or weep tonight,
and give your angels charge over those who sleep;
Tend your sick ones, O Lord Christ, rest your weary
   ones,
bless your dying ones, soothe your suffering ones,
pity your afflicted ones, shield your joyous ones,
and all for your love's sake. Amen.

St Augustine (354–430)

Lord God
You are as mighty as the ocean
As mysterious as the sea
In the storm I called upon you
But I did not see you
I cried out above the waves
But no relief, no help came
I sought for comfort in distress
My faith wavered at each blast
The rocks felt close and dangerous
I asked for healing of my pain
Are you there, Lord?
Are you aware, Lord?
Come walk the waves
Still my storm

David Adam

You who guided Noah over the flood waves:
Hear us.
You who with your word recalled Jonah from the deep:
Deliver us.
You who stretched forth your hand to Peter as he sank:
Help us, O Christ.
Son of God, who did marvellous things of old:
Be favourable in our day also.

Scots Celtic Prayer

How long, O Lord? Will you forget me for ever?
How long will you hide your face from me?
How long must I wrestle with my thoughts
and every day have sorrow in my heart?
How long will my enemy triumph over me?
Look on me and answer, O Lord, my God.
Give light to my eyes, or I will sleep in death;
my enemy will say, 'I have overcome him,'
and my foes will rejoice when I fall.
But I trust in your unfailing love;
my heart rejoices in your salvation.
I will sing to the Lord,
for he has been good to me.

Psalm 13

O God, grant me courage, gaiety of spirit and
tranquillity of mind.

Robert Louis Stevenson (1850–94)

Fill us, we pray, with your light and life, that we may show forth your wondrous glory. Grant that your love may so fill our lives that we may count nothing too small to do for you, nothing too much to give and nothing too hard to bear.

St Ignatius Loyola (1491–1556)

May I be patient! It is so difficult to realize what one believes, and to make these trials, as they are intended, real blessings.

John Henry Newman (1801–90)

Square my trial to my proportioned strength.

John Milton (1608–74)

Grant, O God, that amidst all the discouragements, difficulties, dangers, distress and darkness of this mortal life, I may depend upon thy mercy, and on this build my hopes, as on a sure foundation. Let thine infinite mercy in Christ Jesus deliver me from despair, both now and at the hour of death.

Thomas Wilson (1663–1755)

Peace

O God, from whom all holy desires, all good counsels, and all just works do proceed; give unto thy servants that peace which the world cannot give; that both our hearts may be set to obey thy commandments, and also that by thee we being defended from the fear of our enemies may pass our time in rest and quietness; through the merits of Jesus Christ our Saviour. Amen.

Book of Common Prayer

The Lord bless thee, and keep thee:
The Lord make his face shine upon thee, and be
    gracious unto thee:
The Lord lift up his countenance upon thee, and give
    thee peace.

Numbers 6:24–26

Let us not seek *out* of thee what we can find only *in*
thee, O Lord: peace and rest and joy and bliss, which
abide in thee alone.

Lift up our souls above the weary round of
harassing thoughts to thy eternal presence.

Lift up our minds to the pure, bright, serene light
of thy presence, that there we may repose in thy love
and be at rest from ourselves and all things that
weary us; and thence return, arrayed in thy peace, to
do and to bear whatsoever shall best please thee, O
blessed Lord.

Edward B. Pusey (1800–82)

Deep peace of the running wave to you,
Deep peace of the flowing air to you,
Deep peace of the quiet earth to you,
Deep peace of the shining stars to you,
Deep peace of the Son of Peace to you, for ever.

Source unknown (early Scottish)

O God, make us children of quietness and heirs of peace.

St Clement of Rome (first century)

God our Father, creator of the world,
please help us to love one another.
Make nations friendly with other nations;
make all of us love one another like brothers and
    sisters.
Help us to do our part to bring peace in the world
and happiness to all people.

Prayer from Japan

In thy house, O Lord, let us dwell in peace and
    concord;
give us all one heart, one mind, one true
    interpretation
upon thy word; that all who believe in thee may
    together extol thy name;
O Lord God, most glorious and excellent over all.
Amen.

Godly Prayers (1552)

O almighty God, the Father of all mankind, we pray
thee to turn to thyself the hearts of all peoples and
their rulers, that by the power of thy Holy Spirit
peace may be established on the foundations of
justice, righteousness and truth; through him who
was lifted up on the cross to draw all men unto
himself, even thy Son, Jesus Christ our Lord.

William Temple (1881–1944)

Peace be to this house
and to all who dwell in it.
Peace be to them that enter
and to them that depart.

Anonymous

O God of many names
Lover of all nations
We pray for peace
  in our hearts
  in our homes
  in our nations
  in our world
The peace of your will
The peace of our need.

George Appleton

O Lord, calm the waves of this heart; calm its
tempests. Calm thyself, O my soul, so that the divine
can act in thee. Calm thyself, O my soul, so that God
is able to repose in thee, so that his peace may cover
thee. Yes, Father in heaven, often have we found that
the world cannot give us peace, but make us feel that
thou art able to give peace; let us know the truth of
thy promise: that the whole world may not be able to
take away thy peace.

Søren Kierkegaard (1813–55)

O Lamb of God, that takest away the sins of the world, have mercy upon us.
O Lamb of God, that takest away the sins of the world, have mercy upon us.
O Lamb of God: that takest away the sins of the world, grant us thy peace.

From the Litany, Book of Common Prayer

Lord, hasten the day when nations will beat their swords into plowshares, and their spears into pruninghooks, when nation shall not lift up sword against nation, nor learn war any more.

Based on Micah 4:3

O Lord, the author and persuader of peace, love and goodwill, soften our hard and steely hearts, warm our icy and frozen hearts, that we may wish one another well, and may be the true disciples of Jesus Christ. And give us grace even now to begin to display that heavenly life in which there is no disagreement or hatred, but peace and love on all hands, one towards another.

Ludovicus Vives (1492–1540)

The peace of God be with you,
the peace of Christ be with you,
the peace of Spirit be with you
and with your children,
from the day that we have here today
until the day of the end of your lives.

Celtic prayer

Almighty God, from whom all thoughts of truth and peace proceed, kindle, we pray thee, in the hearts of all men the true love of peace, and guide with thy pure and peaceable wisdom those who take counsel for the nations of the earth; that in tranquillity thy kingdom may go forward, till the earth be filled with the knowledge of thy love; through Jesus Christ our Lord.

Francis Paget (1851–1911)

The blessing of the Lord rest and remain upon all his people, in every land, of every tongue; the Lord meet in mercy all that seek him; the Lord comfort all who suffer and mourn; the Lord hasten his coming, and give us, his people, the blessing of peace.

Handley Moule (1841–1920)

Lord, make me an instrument of your peace.
Where there is hatred, let me sow love;
Where there is injury, pardon;
Where there is discord, union;
Where there is doubt, faith;
Where there is despair, hope;
Where there is darkness, light;
Where there is sadness, joy.

O divine Master, grant that I may not so much seek to be consoled as to console, to be understood as to understand, to be loved as to love;
for it is in giving that we receive,
it is in pardoning that we are pardoned, and
it is in dying that we are born to eternal life.

Attributed to St Francis of Assisi (1181–1226)

We bring before you, O Lord Christ, those whose earthly life is almost at an end. Lessen their fear, encourage them on their journey and give them the peace that comes from your victory over death.

Author unknown

To you, Creator of nature and humanity,
of truth and beauty, I pray:
  Hear my voice,
for it is the voice of the victims of all wars
and violence among individuals and nations.
  Hear my voice,
for it is the voice of all children who suffer and will
    suffer
when people put their faith in weapons and war.
  Hear my voice,
when I beg you to instil into the hearts
of all human beings the wisdom of peace,
the strength of justice and the joy of fellowship.
  Hear my voice,
for I speak for the multitudes in every country
and every period of history who do not want war
and are ready to walk the road of peace.
  Hear my voice,
and grant insight and strength so that we may always
respond to hatred with love, to injustice
with total dedication to justice,
to need with sharing of self, to war with peace.
  O God, hear my voice, and grant unto the world
your everlasting peace.

  Pope John Paul II (1920–2005)

The peace of God, which passeth all understanding, keep your hearts and minds in the knowledge and love of God, and of his Son Jesus Christ our Lord: and the blessing of God Almighty, the Father, the Son, and the Holy Ghost, be amongst you and remain with you always. Amen.

Book of Common Prayer